OLYMPIC
GAMES
2008

China: Host Nation 2008

Melanie Guile

Heinemann
LIBRARY

First published in 2008 by Heinemann Library,
an imprint of Pearson Australia Group Pty Ltd,
20 Thackray Road, Port Melbourne
Victoria 3207 Australia

Visit the Heinemann Library website
www.heinemannlibrary.com.au

Commissioning: Michelle Freeman and Sarah Russell
Editorial: Eliza Collins
Cover and text design: Anne Donald
Map and diagram illustration: Anne Donald
Picture/permissions research: Jes Senbergs and
Wendy Duncan
Production: Tracey Jarrett

Typeset in Syntax 12/17 pt
Pre-press by Publishing Pre-press, Port Melbourne
Printed and bound by Craft Print International
Limited, Singapore
The paper used to print this book comes from
sustainable resources.

**National Library of Australia
Cataloguing-in-Publication data:**

Guile, Melanie, 1949– .
Olympic Games 2008: China: host nation 2008.

Bibliography.
Includes index.
For primary school students.
ISBN 9781740703710 (hbk).

1. Olympic Games (29th : 2008 : Beijing, China) –
Juvenile literature. 2. China - Juvenile literature.
I. Title.

796.48

Acknowledgements
The publisher would like to thank the following for
permission to reproduce copyright material: Corbis/
Tim Davis: p. **27**, /Macduff Everton: p. **16**, /Dave
G Houser: p. **12**, /Imagemore Co: p. **28** (upper),
/Michael S. Yamashita: p. **18**; Getty Images/AFP/Liu
Jin: pp. **7, 21**, /Peter Parks: p. **5**, /Bongarts/Henri
Szwarc: p. **25**, /ChinaFotoPress: pp. **6, 20**, /China
Photos: p. **19**, /John Giustina: p. **29** (centre), /Ross
Kinnaird: p. **24**, /NBAE/Bill Baptist: p. **23**, /Luis Veiga:
p. **29** (lower), /Warner Bros: p. **22**; Lonely Planet
Images/Noboru Komine: p. **29** (upper); photolibrary/
Alamy/BL Images: pp. **13, 28** (lower), /Tibor Bognar:
p. **14**, /Brian Cheung: p. **28** (centre), /James Davis
Photography: p. **8**, /Martin Norris: p. **17**, /Papilio:
p. **26**, /WorldFoto: p. **15**. All other images PhotoDisc.

Cover photograph of the Great Wall of China
reproduced with permission of photolibrary/Alamy/
Brian Cheung.

Every attempt has been made to trace and
acknowledge copyright. Where an attempt has been
unsuccessful, the publisher would be pleased to hear
from the copyright owner so any omission or error
can be rectified.

Disclaimer
All the Internet addresses (URLs) given in this book
were valid at the time of going to press. However,
due to the dynamic nature of the Internet, some
addresses may have changed or ceased to exist
since publication. While the author and publisher
regret any inconvenience this may cause readers, no
responsibility for any such changes can be accepted
by either the author or the publisher.

Contents

Words that are printed in bold, **like this**, are explained in the Glossary on page 31.

Introduction

In August 2008, China will host the 29th summer Olympic Games. This will not only be a chance for China to show its sporting skills to the world. It will also show China as it is today – a rapidly growing power of **industry** with a bright future built on a rich and **ancient** culture.

A huge country

China is a huge country. It has the third largest land area in the world (9.6 million square kilometres) after Canada and Russia. China's population of more than 1.3 **billion** people is the largest on Earth. Most Chinese people are farmers who live in **rural** areas, but things are changing. Factories and industry are growing rapidly. Many people are moving to the cities where there are plenty of jobs and higher **wages**.

Oldest history

China has not only the largest population on Earth, but it also has the oldest written history, whereby scholars recorded important dates and events. Chinese history goes back more than 4000 years to 2000 BCE. For many centuries, powerful ruling families, called **dynasties**, ran the country. Many dynasties ruled for hundreds of years. Beautiful pottery, paintings, poetry and music were produced. Chinese silk, porcelain – or china – and tea were traded around the world. China became one nation under **Emperor** Qin Shi Huang Di in 221 BCE.

China fact file

Name People's Republic of China

Land area 9 572 900 square kilometres

Capital city Beijing

Independence 1949

Government Communist republic

Leader President Hu Jintao

Population 1 321 851 888
      (estimated July 2007)

Official language Mandarin Chinese

Money Renminbi (RMB) (the **yuan**)

Then, in the 1800s, China was **invaded** by Europeans and fell into a chaos of hunger, drug-dealing and fighting warlords. The last emperor was thrown out by popular leader, Sun Yatsen, in 1911. War continued until the **communists** took over in 1949 and brought peace to China.

Government

Since 1949, the Chinese people have been ruled by the Communist Party and its president. The people cannot vote for anyone else in elections. In a communist country, farms, industries and businesses are run by the government and wealth is shared equally. But, since the 1980s, people have been allowed to run their own businesses in China. As a result, the number of rich people has grown, and the cities are booming. However, people in rural areas have become poorer as government money and support has gone to the cities, and pollution and **corruption** are major problems. This has led some groups in China, such as students and lawyers, to call for more freedom and **democracy**.

The red background on China's flag stands for courage. The yellow stars stand for the four groups of people – workers, farmers, middle classes and the rich – equal under the one rule of the Communist Party.

The 91 000-seat National Stadium in China's capital, Beijing, is one of 12 new venues being built for the Olympic Games in 2008.

5

China and the Olympic Games

Since attending its first Olympic Games in 1932, China has become one of the world's best Olympic nations. At the Beijing Olympic Games in 2008, China hopes to top the medal table. It has every chance of doing so because of the money and effort the government has put into training and sports in recent years.

The modern Olympic Games

The first modern Olympic Games were held in Athens, Greece, in 1896. They were an international sporting competition modelled on the **ancient** Greek games held over 2000 years ago. The organiser and 'father of the modern Olympics', Baron Pierre de Coubertin, invited all countries to the Olympic Games. He sent an invitation to China, but there was no reply.

Chinese interest

During the 1920s, interest in international sporting competitions grew in China. In 1932, China sent its first Olympic athlete, sprinter Liu Changchun, to the Los Angeles Games in the USA. Chinese athletes competed in the Olympic Games until 1949, when the **communists** established the People's **Republic** of China. Taiwan, an island off the mainland, became **anti-communist** Nationalist China – so there were 'two Chinas'.

The new National Aquatics Centre in Beijing, known as the 'Water Cube', will house Olympic swimming and diving events in 2008. It was designed and engineered by Australians.

The 'two Chinas' problem

For almost 20 years, Taiwan competed in the Olympic Games as 'China', but the much larger People's Republic of China did not compete. However, in 1979, the International Olympic Committee (IOC) encouraged the Communist People's Republic to rejoin the Olympic Games.

Olympic success

The 1984 Los Angeles Olympic Games in the USA were Communist China's first games in 20 years. The Chinese team won 15 gold, eight silver and nine bronze medals and came fourth in the medal tally. Since then, China has done well in shooting, swimming, diving, gymnastics and table tennis.

At the Athens Olympic Games in Greece in 2004, China won 32 gold medals. This was the second highest number after the USA, which won 36 gold medals.

The Beijing bid

In February 2000, China made a **bid**, or offer, to host the Olympic Games in Beijing. Other finalists for the games were Toronto (Canada), Paris (France), Istanbul (Turkey) and Osaka (Japan). Beijing was the favourite, although some people believed China's pollution and poor **human rights** record would damage its chances. However, on 13 July 2001, the IOC awarded the 2008 Olympic Games to Beijing.

Champion hurdler Liu Xiang (left) won the 110 metres hurdles at the Athens Olympic Games in 2004 and became a national hero. As the world's fastest hurdler, Liu is an excellent chance for gold in this event at Beijing.

China's Olympic medal tally

China has achieved much success in its short Olympic Games history. Since 1979, China has won:

- 112 gold, 96 silver, 78 bronze in six summer Olympic Games;

- two gold, 12 silver, eight bronze in seven winter Olympic Games;

- 133 gold medals in six Paralympic Games. China topped the medal tally at the 2004 Paralympic Games in Athens, Greece.

The land

Beijing is China's capital. It is in the north-east of the country. Many visitors will enjoy touring Beijing during the Olympic Games, but they will see only a tiny part of the huge country that is China. The land stretches more than 5000 kilometres from the western mountains and deserts to the eastern coastline. It is another 5000 kilometres from the cold grassy plains of the north to the tropical south. China has some of the highest and lowest places on Earth, and the coldest and hottest climates.

Environmental problems

China has significant problems with pollution. This can perhaps be linked to China's huge population and the rapid increase in **industry** and development.

- Seven out of ten of the world's most polluted cities are in China.
- China is the world's worst air polluter.
- One-third of China's land is spoiled by over use.
- Half of the Chinese people do not have clean drinking water.
- China has signed the **Kyoto Protocol**, which is an international agreement to cut the **greenhouse gases** that cause the Earth to heat up. However, China does not have to cut greenhouse gases under that agreement because it is one of the poorer or 'developing' countries.

Many visitors to Beijing during the Olympic Games will no doubt visit the Forbidden City, which was the Chinese imperial palace for many centuries.

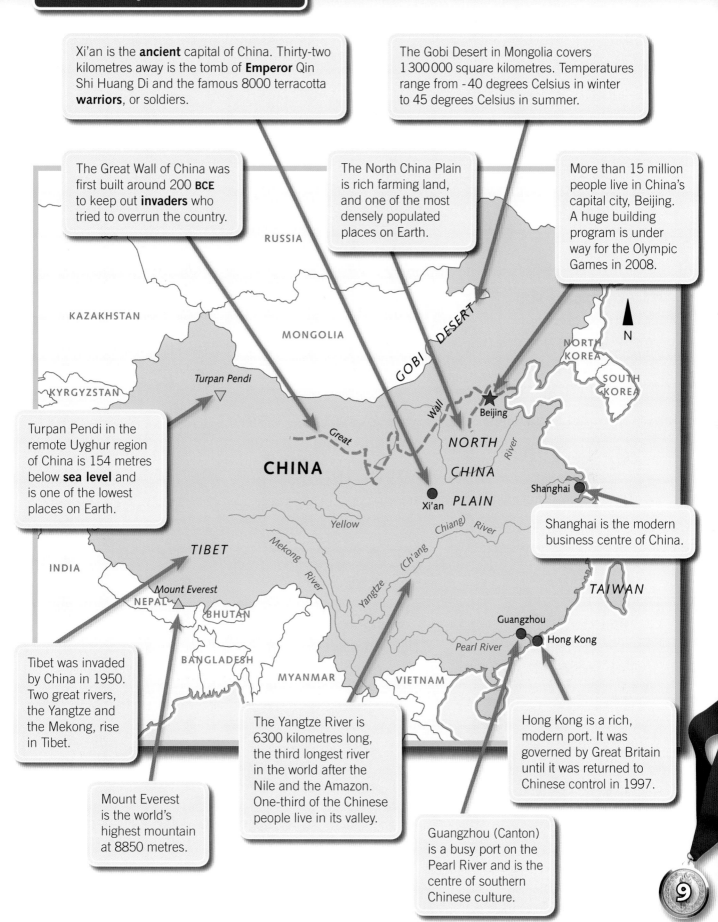

Xi'an is the **ancient** capital of China. Thirty-two kilometres away is the tomb of **Emperor** Qin Shi Huang Di and the famous 8000 terracotta **warriors**, or soldiers.

The Gobi Desert in Mongolia covers 1 300 000 square kilometres. Temperatures range from -40 degrees Celsius in winter to 45 degrees Celsius in summer.

The Great Wall of China was first built around 200 **BCE** to keep out **invaders** who tried to overrun the country.

The North China Plain is rich farming land, and one of the most densely populated places on Earth.

More than 15 million people live in China's capital city, Beijing. A huge building program is under way for the Olympic Games in 2008.

Turpan Pendi in the remote Uyghur region of China is 154 metres below **sea level** and is one of the lowest places on Earth.

Shanghai is the modern business centre of China.

Tibet was invaded by China in 1950. Two great rivers, the Yangtze and the Mekong, rise in Tibet.

The Yangtze River is 6300 kilometres long, the third longest river in the world after the Nile and the Amazon. One-third of the Chinese people live in its valley.

Hong Kong is a rich, modern port. It was governed by Great Britain until it was returned to Chinese control in 1997.

Mount Everest is the world's highest mountain at 8850 metres.

Guangzhou (Canton) is a busy port on the Pearl River and is the centre of southern Chinese culture.

RUSSIA

KAZAKHSTAN

MONGOLIA

GOBI DESERT

NORTH KOREA

SOUTH KOREA

N

KYRGYZSTAN

Turpan Pendi

Great Wall

Beijing

NORTH CHINA PLAIN

River

CHINA

Xi'an

Shanghai

Yellow

Chiang River

TIBET

Mekong River

(Ch'ang)

Yangtze

INDIA

Mount Everest

NEPAL

BHUTAN

TAIWAN

BANGLADESH

MYANMAR

VIETNAM

Guangzhou

Pearl River

Hong Kong

History of China timeline

China is one of the longest settled countries on Earth. Its history spans many thousands of years, during which the Chinese developed one of the world's richest cultures.

Before 5000 BCE
Stone Age people settle in villages in northern China.

Around 2000 BCE
The 17 kings of the Xia period rule in northern China.

Around 1700–1100 BCE
The first written records are kept during the Shang period.

Around 1100–221 BCE
Iron is used to make weapons during the Zhou period.

551–479 BCE
The great thinker, Confucius, lives. His ideas on how to live a better life lead to the Chinese religion of **Confucianism**.

221–206 BCE
The Qin **Dynasty**. China becomes a nation under the first **Emperor** Qin Shi Huang Di. He builds the Great Wall of China and is buried with the famous terracotta warriors.

202 BCE–220 AD
The Han Dynasty enjoys 400 years of peaceful rule. The capital is at Xi'an.

220–280 AD
The Three Kingdoms period brings warfare.

Around 300–600 AD
Barbarians from the north **invade** and rule China.

618–907 AD
The Tang Dynasty is a golden age of peace, wealth and culture. Printing is invented, and the **Buddhist** religion comes to China.

960–1279 AD
During the Song Dynasty, great art and literature are produced. The compass, gunpowder and **movable type** for printing are invented.

1215
Genghis Khan and the Mongols capture Beijing and set up the Yuan Dynasty.

1275–1292
Italian Marco Polo becomes the first European visitor to China.

1368–1644
Europeans arrive in China during the Ming Dynasty. The capital is moved to Beijing where the Forbidden City is built for the emperor.

1644–1911

Invaders from the north set up the Manchu Dynasty. The Summer Palace is built in Beijing. European countries overpower China.

26 December 1893

Mao Zedong, the future leader of **Communist** China, is born.

1911

Sun Yatsen throws out the last Manchu emperor and sets up a **republic**.

1937

Japan invades China.

1945

Japan is defeated.

1945–1949

Civil war erupts. Mao Zedong's communists fight the Nationalist Army led by Chiang Kai-shek.

1949

The communists win and set up the People's Republic of China led by Mao Zedong. All properties, farms and businesses are owned by the state. Chairman Mao becomes a godlike figure.

1966–1976

The **Cultural Revolution** is started by Mao. Many people die, and artworks and historic buildings are destroyed.

9 September 1976

Mao Zedong dies.

1977

Deng Xiaoping takes control. He encourages people to run their own businesses and make money.

1989

Students demonstrate for **democracy** in Tiananmen Square, Beijing, and are crushed by tanks and government troops.

1997

Deng Xiaoping dies. Jiang Zemin becomes leader.

2001

Beijing is awarded the right to host the Olympic Games in 2008.

2003

Jiang Zemin steps down as leader. Hu Jintao becomes president. China becomes the fastest growing economy in the world.

2008

China hosts the 29th summer Olympic Games.

11

The people

China's people are united by a strong central government and a common written language. But there are growing differences – between city and country, new and old, and rich and poor. The Chinese Government aims to bring the people together as they celebrate the hosting of the Olympic Games in 2008.

Ethnic groups

The Han Chinese are the largest **ethnic group** in China. They make up around 93 per cent of the population. Han Chinese are found in all parts of the country, but most live on the rich plains of the Yellow and Yangtze rivers.

Fifty-six other ethnic groups, known as 'national minorities', live mainly near China's borders. These include the Uyghurs in central Asia, the Mongolians in the far north-west, and the Miao people in the south-west. Although controlled by the government in Beijing, China's ethnic groups try to maintain their traditional ways of life.

Languages

Mandarin Chinese is the official language of the People's Republic of China. It is based on the language spoken in northern China. In other parts of the country, Chinese people speak **dialects**. Cantonese is the best known of these. The 56 ethnic groups generally speak their own languages, but schools teach Mandarin.

Chinese writing is based on **pictographs**, which are simple pictures used to represent a word. There are up to 56 000 different pictographs, but most people can read around 6000.

The Miao ethnic group wear spectacular traditional costumes. More than 7 million Miao live in **remote** mountain regions in the south-west of China. They are closely related to the Hmong people of Thailand and Vietnam.

Say it in Mandarin Chinese

Sound out the words as they are spelt.

Hello	*say*	'nee hao'		I'm thirsty	*say*	'wo ker-la'
Good morning		'zao an'		Do you understand?		'nee ming bai ma?'
Good night		'wan an'		Yes		'shi'
What is your name?		'nin gwee-xing'		No		'boo shi'
My (sur)name is …		'wo xing'		Thank you		'xie-air xie-air'
I'm hungry.		'wo wer-la'				

City and country

Most Chinese live in **rural** areas and work on farms. Many people are poor. They work hard in the fields and eat mostly rice and vegetables. School is cheap, but many children – especially girls – finish only primary school because they are needed to work on the family farm. Houses are usually one-roomed concrete blocks with no flushing toilets or running water. Half of all household water in China is polluted.

But all this is changing. Young people are flocking to the cities where **wages** are better and living is easier. Modern high-rise apartments, restaurants, entertainment and high-tech **industries** attract country people. Today, almost 40 per cent of Chinese people live in the cities, and that number is growing every year.

Modern, wealthy Shanghai has cafes, fashionable shops and a lively music scene.

The people

The Communist Government once controlled almost every part of people's lives. In recent years, however, laws have softened, leading some people to call for more freedom, but the battle is far from over.

Religion

China has no state religion, and for many years all religions were banned. Today, however, religious belief is growing. There are three traditional religions in China – **Taoism**, **Confucianism** and **Buddhism**.

Taoism was started around 650 BCE, and is China's oldest religion. It is based on the idea of living in **harmony** with natural powers. Confucianism is a set of rules for living written by Confucius around 500 BCE. They stress duty and obedience and respect for family and **elders**. Buddhism spread from India to China in about 300 AD. It teaches the 'path to **enlightenment'**, or understanding and happiness, through careful thoughts, words and deeds. **Islam** is strong among **ethnic groups** in western China. **Christians** make up about one per cent of the population.

Buddhists attend a **temple**. The **communists** banned all religions in 1949, but a law passed in 1982 promised freedom of religion.

Falun Gong

The **Falun Gong** is a religious group linked to Buddhism. In 1999, the group rallied in Beijing for freedom to follow its beliefs. The government banned the group and put many Falun Gong members in jail. **Human rights** groups around the world **condemned** China's treatment of them and other protesters.

China's population is still growing rapidly, but the government aims to keep it under 1.5 **billion**. Until 2006, couples in Shanghai were paid money not to have children.

One child policy

With 1.3 billion people, China has a population problem. In 1979, the government introduced the One Child Policy of only one child per family to keep numbers down. Unrest in the **rural** areas, where large families are traditional, led the government to soften the law. Now, rural families are allowed two babies.

Boys are believed to be better than girls in China, and many families make sure their only child is male. Girl babies are sometimes killed for this reason. This has led to more boys being born than girls. In China today, nearly 120 boys are born for every 100 girls, leading to a shortage of women for men to marry. In some parts of China, young women have been kidnapped from their families to be brides.

Families

Old people are highly respected in Chinese culture. Children obey their parents and ask them for advice about schooling, work and marriage. Traditionally, adult children look after their older relatives. But the One Child Policy means that there is only one child to care for two aged parents and four grandparents. This puts a strain on the family. By 2040, there will be 400 million old people to care for. The government is looking at ways to tackle the problem.

Food

China is famous for its wonderful food. Visitors to the Beijing Olympic Games will find a huge variety of dishes to try, from fast food hamburgers to traditional Chinese treats like monkeys' brains or shark's fin soup.

Changing tastes

Like everything else in China today, food choices are changing. Most people prefer traditional food, such as noodles or rice, with meat or seafood and plenty of fresh vegetables cooked in delicious sauces. But, in modern cities like Beijing and Shanghai, restaurants serve food from all over the world. Young people are also developing a taste for hamburgers, pizzas and soft drinks.

Traditional food

There are many styles of cooking in China that are based on the regions they come from. Cantonese food comes from the south coast of China where there is plenty of seafood and rice. Vegetables are eaten with unusual meats, including snake, monkey and dog. Food is chopped and steamed or stir-fried in sauces with ginger, lemon grass and other herbs added for flavour. Rice is eaten with every meal.

Northern style

The northern style of Chinese cooking is centred on Beijing. It is richer than Cantonese food to suit the colder climate. Thick, tasty beef stews and roasted lamb are popular. Rice does not grow in the dry north, so wheat is used to make dumplings and noodles. Beijing's most famous dish is Peking duck. This is made up of crisp-skinned roasted duck served with pancakes, onions and sour plum sauce.

Diners take a piece of Peking duck, dip it in sauce, add onion and wrap it in the pancake.

Beijing street stalls sell 250 types of traditional snack foods. For example, instant-boiled mutton – strips of lamb dipped in boiling water and served with sauces – is a winter favourite.

Sichuan style

Hot and spicy Sichuan food comes from the area around Chengdu in south-central China. Fiery red chillies, garlic, pepper and ginger are stir-fried with pork, duck or chicken and vegetables to make mouth-wateringly tasty dishes. Meats are often soaked in spicy sauces before cooking to add to the flavour.

Egg drop soup

This Cantonese-style soup is not too spicy.

Ingredients

1 litre chicken stock	2 eggs, lightly beaten
½ teaspoon grated fresh ginger	2 spring onions, chopped
1 tablespoon soy sauce	salt and pepper
1 tablespoon cornflour	

Method

1 Heat the stock, ginger and soy sauce in a saucepan.

2 Mix the cornflour with two tablespoons of the stock to make a paste. Slowly add it to the boiling stock, and stir until it thickens. Reduce heat.

3 Pour in eggs while slowly stirring the soup. Turn off heat.

4 Add spring onions and salt and pepper to taste.

Customs and traditions

Life in China is changing rapidly. Some people worry that the old ways are disappearing, but many traditional customs remain strong.

Family life

Family is still the centre of people's lives. Grandparents live with their adult children and often look after the baby while the parents work. Meals are a time for the family to relax together. Dead **ancestors**, or relatives who died a long time ago, are remembered and their graves are looked after.

However, with many adult children leaving their villages to work in cities, family bonds are weakening. Traditionally, fathers, husbands and older brothers had control over the lives of their female relatives, but this is changing, too. Now, women in modern China often hold important jobs and lead their own lives.

'Saving face'

'Saving face' means not being shamed, or embarrassed, in public. It is very important in Chinese daily life. People dislike looking foolish and avoid making others appear wrong. In China, it is rude to argue, get angry, or say no. People prefer to talk things over politely. Showing respect is important, especially to teachers and older people. School children behave themselves and study hard because failing shames the family.

On Tomb Sweeping Day in April, people look after their dead relatives' graves and burn paper money for them. Respect for ancestors is weakening in modern China.

The Lantern Festival is held on the first full moon of the year. The lanterns are often decorated with lucky designs.

Celebrations

The Chinese year is filled with wonderful traditional festivals. The biggest holiday is *Chun Jie* (Spring Festival), or Chinese New Year, which takes place in January or February. People clean their houses, buy new clothes, pay all their bills and travel home to share meals with their families. There are 12 animals in the Chinese calendar. Each year is linked to an animal – such as a pig, monkey or dragon – and each animal has special qualities. The year of the Beijing Olympic Games – 2008 – will be the Year of the Rat, a very good year for success in business.

The Lantern Festival (*Yuanxiao Jie*) is held each February. People buy paper lanterns in beautiful colours and shapes, such as dragons and fish, and take them into the parks after dark. The effect is magical.

The Moon Festival

The Moon, or Mid-Autumn, Festival is held in August or September. People eat special 'moon' cakes, and lovers walk together under the full moon. The Moon Festival is held in honour of Chang-e, the moon goddess. Here is her story.

Once upon a time, the hero, Yi, lived with his wife, Chang-e. At that time, there were ten suns in the sky, which scorched the world. Yi shot nine of them down with his bow and arrow and was rewarded by heaven with three pills meant to give long life. Chang-e swallowed all three pills. She turned into a goddess and went to live in the moon where you can still see her face.

Music, dance and art

The Chinese have **ancient** traditions of music, dance and art that the Chinese Government strongly supports. However, tastes are changing. Modern artists, musicians and dancers are trying out new ideas – with a distinct Chinese influence.

Traditional music

Traditional Chinese instruments include flutes, strings, kettle drums and cymbals. Players use difficult rhythms to make haunting melodies. Chinese Opera combines **acrobatics**, dance, singing and an orchestra. It features richly costumed singers playing out ancient stories in a formal style. Western-style classical music and opera are also popular in China, and concerts are always well attended.

Modern music

Young people prefer 'soft pop' or rock music. Idols like Lin Yilun also star in stage and television shows, and in 2005, millions of people voted for Chinese pop singer, Li Yuchun, in the television program, 'Super Girl'. Beijing is home to rock legend Cui Jian whose protest songs called for **democracy** in 1989. In Shanghai and Guangzhou, clubs and dance halls play every kind of music from jazz to hard rock to rap.

Dance

Han Chinese folk dances can be slow and graceful, or wild with leaps and spins. Dancers wear magnificent costumes and often twirl ribbons or flags to make beautiful shapes in the air. Western-style dances are popular in the cities. The Beijing Dance Academy is one of the world's best ballet schools, and modern dances are also popular.

Chinese 'Super Girl' winner Li Yuchun performs. Her website has received more than one **billion** hits. The Chinese Government tries – unsuccessfully – to discourage modern, American-style entertainment.

Folk dances

China's 56 **ethnic groups** have many traditional folk dances, which they perform at festivals or on holy days. For example, the Dai people in southern Yunnan Province perform the Peacock Dance at their Water-Splashing Festival. Graceful arm shapes and leg movements suggest the proud peacock walk and its spreading tail.

Master of ceremonies

Award-winning filmmaker Zhang Yimou will direct the opening and closing ceremonies at the Beijing Olympic Games. He has promised a 'celebration of life' through music, dance and art. Zhang has directed some well-known films, such as *Raise the Red Lantern* (1992) and *House of Flying Daggers* (2004).

Art

Traditional Chinese painting is known for its clear, simple beauty. Artists worked on silk or paper with coloured inks. Landscapes, animals and portraits were popular subjects. In China today, both ancient and modern styles of art are popular. Artist Chen Yifei (1946–2005) was one of China's most famous modern oil painters. His realistic, beautifully painted portraits are in galleries around the world. **Abstract** – or non-realistic – paintings and **multimedia** works – featuring computers and other electronic forms of communication – are shown in Beijing and Shanghai galleries.

In the Dragon Dance, performers become the 'legs' and copy the weaving movements of the dragon.

Sport

Sport has always been important in China. Traditional sports, such as tai chi, are still practised every day for health and long life. Modern team sports and international competitions, however, have only become popular in China in the last 30 years. Today, China is one of the world's top sporting nations.

Traditional sports

More than 2000 years ago, Chinese people invented *cuju*, a kind of football played with a round leather ball stuffed with hair. Wrestling, polo, archery, gymnastics, weightlifting and row boat racing were all popular sports in **ancient** China. But the best known traditional Chinese sports are the **martial arts**, or self-defence sports, such as kung fu and tai chi.

Martial arts

Martial arts were invented hundreds of years ago to train soldiers to defend themselves, but they became popular as sports. There are many different types of martial arts. Some, such as tai chi, involve slow controlled movements, deep breathing and graceful poses. Others, such as kung fu, involve leaps, kicks and weapons such as sticks and knives.

Birthplace of football

In 2004, the Federation of International Football Associations (FIFA) officially recognised *cuju*, an ancient type of Chinese soccer, as the first football game in the world. This means China is the birthplace of football (soccer).

Jet Li is a famous kung fu expert and movie star. Kung fu films and comics are very popular in China.

Modern sports

Football (soccer) is China's most-watched sport. Around 200 million viewers tune in to watch local and international league games on television every week. However, most towns do not have space for soccer pitches, so few people play.

Basketball is the most popular sport in China with 300 million players. Games of the American National Basketball Association (NBA) are screened weekly on television and have a huge fan base, especially among teenagers. Families enjoy games of table tennis and badminton, and many people practise martial arts. Chinese athletes also do well at sports such as swimming, diving, shooting and golf, but these are too expensive for ordinary people to play.

Training for Beijing

In the lead-up to the Beijing Olympic Games, the Chinese Government has put lots of money and effort into sports training programs. Now, China has the world's top diving team, which won six gold medals at the Athens Olympic Games in 2004.

The Chinese are also Olympic champions in weightlifting, shooting, badminton and table tennis. Judo, tennis, snooker and women's volleyball are strong sports for China internationally too.

Basketball player Yao Ming is an idol among teenage boys. At 2.3 metres tall and highly talented, Yao was selected to play for the NBA in the USA.

23

Sport

In recent years, China has poured a great deal of money and energy into a wide range of sports. School children, winter sport athletes and people with disabilities have all benefited from government support.

Sport in schools

Physical education programs are run in Chinese schools, but sports facilities are limited by lack of space. Chinese children love football (soccer), but few schools have playing fields. However, most schools play basketball, and gymnastics and badminton are popular with girls. Many children play table tennis for fun.

Sports schools

About 360 000 students attend special government-run sports schools in China, which teach a wide range of Olympic sports. Children are selected at the age of seven, and train for long hours every day. Around 100 000 trained athletes are turned out by sports schools every year, providing a huge pool of sporting talent for the Olympics and other international competitions.

Diver Fu Mingxia went to sports school at seven, and won her first world title, aged 12. She won Olympic gold three times – in Barcelona in 1992, Atlanta in 1996 and Sydney in 2000 – with almost perfect dives from the 10 metre and 3 metre boards.

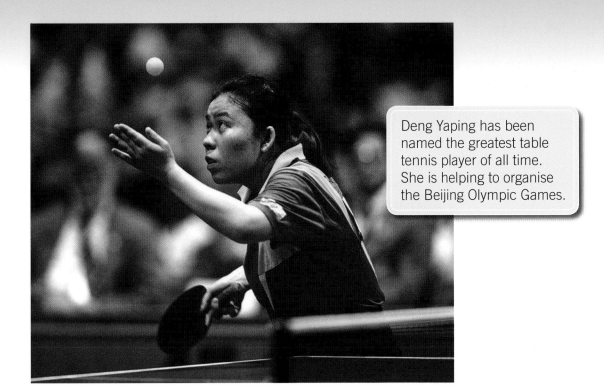

Deng Yaping has been named the greatest table tennis player of all time. She is helping to organise the Beijing Olympic Games.

Table tennis

Table tennis was invented in England in the late 1800s, but soon became very popular in China, where approximately 200 million people play the sport today. Not surprisingly, China tops the world in the sport. Wang Liqin is the world's top-ranking table tennis player, but he has never won Olympic gold. China's all-time table tennis great is Deng Yaping. She has won 18 world championships and four Olympic gold medals – two each in Barcelona in 1992 and Atlanta in 1996. In 2003, Deng was voted Athlete of the Century in China.

Winter Olympic Games

In 1980, China sent its first winter Olympic team to Lake Placid in the USA and has competed ever since. Speed skater Ye Qiaobo won China's first winter Olympic medal – a silver – in 1992 in Albertville, France. In 2002, China won its first winter Olympic Games gold for speed skating in Salt Lake City, USA. China is strong in speed skating, skiing and women's ice hockey.

Paralympic Games

Just 24 athletes with disabilities attended China's first Paralympic Games, held jointly in New York (USA) and Stoke Mandeville (England) in 1984. The team won 22 medals overall, including two gold. Training and facilities for disabled athletes improved in China during the 1990s. In 2004, China sent 200 athletes to the Athens Paralympic Games. The team won 63 gold medals and finished second overall to the USA. China aims to beat the rest of the world at the Beijing Paralympic Games in 2008.

Animals

Many wonderful animals – including bears, tigers, leopards, monkeys and deer – live in China. But they compete for living space and food with more than 1.3 **billion** people, and the animals are losing the struggle to survive.

The giant panda

Giant pandas are medium-sized bears that are around 150 centimetres long and weigh up to 150 kilograms. They live in **remote** mountain forests in south-west China and feed only on bamboo. Giant pandas are **protected** by law, and must not be hunted. More than 50 reserves, or special areas of land, have been set aside for them in China. Today, only 1600 giant pandas are left in the wild.

The double fur coat serves two purposes: the outer fur is oily to keep the panda dry; the thick woolly inner fur is for warmth in the snowy mountain winters.

Strong jaws and large flat teeth are designed for chewing tough bamboo stalks.

The special wrist bone acts like a thumb with which the panda grabs and cuts bamboo stalks.

The giant panda uses its sharp claws for climbing trees if in danger.

Black and white markings make the panda hard to see in the shadows of the forest.

Endangered

Many Chinese animals are **endangered** and at risk of dying out. Water pollution and land clearing mean that animals have nowhere safe to live. Bears, tigers and snow leopards are killed by hunters who sell the body parts for traditional medicines.

China's most endangered animal is the Yangtze dolphin. This pale grey dolphin lives in the Yangtze River, which is very polluted and clogged with ships. The dolphins get caught in fishing nets because their direction-finding system is damaged by noise from motor boats. No Yangtze dolphin has been seen since 2004, and some people think it is already **extinct**.

Saving the animals

It is not all bad news for the animals, however. The Chinese Government is setting aside land, called reserves, for them. For example, the Huichun National Reserve has been created in forests near the Korean border to save north-east tigers and snow leopards from dying out. Also, zoos are breeding endangered animals – such the south China tiger, the oxlike takin and the Chinese alligator – and numbers are slowly increasing.

The south China tiger is one of the rarest animals in the world. Only about 40 of them are left in Chinese zoos.

Olympic mascots

Since 1972, each Olympic Games has had at least one **mascot**. Beijing has chosen the giant panda as one of its five Olympic mascots – called 'The Friendlies' – because it is China's best-known and loved animal. The giant panda mascot, Jingjing, represents happiness. His headdress is made of leaves from the lotus, a plant that stands for purity and perfection in Chinese culture. The other mascots are Yingying, a Tibetan antelope, or deer; Beibei the fish; Nini, a golden-winged swallow; and Huanhuan the Olympic flame.

Postcards from China

Thousands of visitors will flock to Beijing in 2008 to watch the Olympic Games and enjoy what China has to offer. Some people will travel beyond Beijing to visit spectacular tourist spots. Here are just some of the sites.

★ The Temple of Heaven, Beijing ★

Visited the **Temple** of Heaven this morning. It was built in 1420 during the Ming **Dynasty**. The round building is the Hall of Prayer for Good Harvests where the **emperor** used to pray. It stands on a marble terrace and the steps up to it are covered in carvings.

★ The Great Wall of China, Badaling ★

Travelled 70 kilometres by bus today to see the Great Wall of China. This is the nearest part of the wall to Beijing and it is crowded with tourists. The wall was built more than 2000 years ago to keep out foreign **invaders**. It used to stretch for 5000 kilometres, but only small sections are left now. We walked along the top of the wall, but it was very steep in places!

★ The terracotta army, near Xi'an ★

Started our tour yesterday by flying to Xi'an, then drove out to see the terracotta **warriors**. They were buried 2000 years ago in the tomb of Emperor Qin Shi Huang Di. There are 8000 life-sized clay solders standing ready for battle. Each one is carrying a crossbow, spear or axe. They look so lifelike.

★ Cloud Ridge Caves, near Datong ★

Arrived in Datong today and took a minibus to the Cloud Ridge Caves just outside town. The caves were carved out of a cliff face around 490 **AD** to make **Buddhist** temples. They are decorated with 50 000 amazing sculptures of Buddhas and gods.

★ Huang Shan Mountains, Anhui Province ★

Stopped off on our flight to Shanghai to take in the mysterious Huang Shan Mountains. It's a beautiful place – spectacular peaks, wonderful views, misty valleys, twisted pine trees. The mountains look like a Chinese silk painting.

★ The modern city of Shanghai ★

Spent the last two days in Shanghai. What a buzz this place has – street cafes, clubs, huge shopping malls, stylish couples walking the Bund, which is a famous street on the waterfront. Spent hours looking at beautiful pottery and artworks in the fabulous modern Shanghai Museum.

See you soon!

Find out more

Using the Internet

Explore the Internet to learn more about the people, places and customs featured in this book. Websites can change so if the links below no longer work, use a reliable search engine, such as http://yahooligans.yahoo.com or http://www.kids.net.au, and type in the keywords, such as the name of a person, place or event.

Websites

http://en.beijing2008.cn
The official website of the Beijing Olympic Games covers every aspect of the games, including athlete profiles, sports, venues, cultural information, the latest news and dozens of links. It also features an education section for school children.

www.kidzworld.com/article/1049-olympics-head-to-china-in-2008
This is a user-friendly children's site with interesting information on the Beijing Olympic Games plus links.

http://english.people.com.cn
The website of the official Chinese newspaper, *The People's Daily*, includes a useful 'China at a Glance' page, plus information on Chinese sporting achievements in the last 50 years. Remember, however, that the information on this site is government controlled and may not be objective.

Books

Goddard, C. *China* Evans Publishing, London, 2004
This book examines China's important industries, geography, environment and people, including the ways in which Chinese people spend their leisure time.

Guile, M. *Culture in China* Heinemann Library, Port Melbourne, 2003
This text provides a detailed description of modern Chinese culture, covering daily life, the roles of women, the arts and ethnic groups.

Luh, S. Shin *The People of China* Mason Crest Publishers, Broomall, PA, 2006
This book provides a detailed look at the people living in the world's most populated country, including their beliefs, history, customs and hopes.

Glossary

abstract not realistic-looking

acrobatics an energetic form of gymnastics

AD stands for *Anno Domini* ('in the year of the Lord'). Year 1 is the traditional birth of Jesus Christ. The year 2000 AD is 2000 years after the birth of Christ

ancestor a relative who died a long time ago

ancient in a time long past

anti-communist a person or organisation against communism

barbarians rough and uncivilised people

BCE stands for 'before the common (current) era'. Year 1 is the traditional birth of Jesus Christ. BCE years are the years before year 1, and are counted backwards; for example, 1300 BCE is 1300 years before the birth of Christ.

bid to offer or put in a claim for something

billion one thousand times a million

Buddhism a religion that follows the teachings of the Buddha

Christian a person who believes in the teachings of Christ

communist a person who believes in a political system in which most property is publicly owned and each person works for the benefit of all in the community or state

condemned blamed or made a judgement against someone

Confucianism a religion based on the ideas of Confucius

corruption bad or criminal acts by government officials or other powerful people

Cultural Revolution a campaign by Mao Zedong to enforce the strict rules of the communist revolution. Thousands of artists, writers and teachers were killed or imprisoned, and many cultural treasures were destroyed.

democracy a system of government in which leaders are elected by the people

dialect a form of speech belonging to a particular area or group of people

dynasty a ruling family whose power is passed down through the generations

elder a senior member of the community

emperor a ruler of an empire

endangered likely to become extinct and die out

enlightenment understanding and happiness

ethnic group a group of people from a different country or culture

extinct a species of plant or animal that has died out

Falun Gong a religious group that is banned in China

greenhouse gases gases given off by cars, houses and factories that cause temperatures to rise on Earth

harmony peace and order

human rights rights and freedoms owed to all human beings

industry trade and manufacturing

invaded seized control of a country or state by force

Islam a religion that follows the teachings of Mohammed

Kyoto Protocol an international agreement controlling the amount of greenhouse gases countries can produce

martial arts self-defence sports

mascot a person or thing that brings good luck

movable type a way of printing that uses wooden or metal letters (or Chinese characters) that can be moved about to form different words or sentences for each new printing job

multimedia made up of different media, specifically electronic forms of communication, such as computers

pictograph a picture-symbol used in written language

protected (animals) must not be harmed or killed by law

remote far away

republic a state in which government is carried out by representatives of the people

rural in the country, not the city

sea level height of land at sea shore level

Stone Age a culture from ancient times in which people used only stone, not metal, tools

Taoism a religion based on the teachings of Lao Tsze

temple a building for prayer or worship

wages money paid for work

warrior a soldier

yuan currency, or money, used in China

Index